**SLOW DANCING
TO
MOOD INDIGO**

by Jerry Sexton

Other Books by Jerry Sexton

Poetry:
A Muse for Herbie Lucid

Prose:
SNIPPETS: Overheard Conversations and Other Short Short Fiction Pieces

available on Amazon.com

SLOW DANCING TO MOOD INDIGO

by Jerry Sexton

Poetry by Jerry Sexton

Copyright © 2019 by Jerry Sexton

Lionel A. Blanchard, Publisher,
Santa Clara, CA

All rights reserved. No part of this publication may be reproduced, stored in a retrieval system, or transmitted, in any form or by any means, electronic, mechanical, photocopying, recording, or otherwise, without the prior written permission of the author.

First Printing

ISBN: 978-1-7335858-0-4

Printed in the United States of America

Dedication

I only began writing poetry at the age of thirty-five. I am indebted to poets with whom I have studied in the past, particularly Edward L. Meyerson, Robert Hass, Richard Maxwell, Frances Mayes, Alan Soldofsky, Samuel Maio, and Ishmael Reed. I would also like to thank my publisher, Lionel A. Blanchard, who has continued to be a supportive friend for decades. This book is dedicated to him.

Contents

[Our Holding, a Holding On,]	1
The Master Plan	2
A Thank-You Note	3
A Resolution of Distance	4
A Day in San Francisco	5
What Remains	7
An Explanation to Consider	8
For Greater Commiseration	9
Description of a Physical State	10
One Solution	11
Distancing	12
Dobie Gillis at the Easel	13
Salamma Lamma	14
Untitled	15
Fragments	16
What I Tell You as You Dance	17
Think-Feel	18
What It Is	19
She's Going to Make It	20
Keeping On	21
Doing Sad	22
Our Having Known Each Other for Some Time Now	23

For Your Consideration	24
One Poet–An Update	25
This I Do for Myself	29
To The Girl with the Golden Eyes	30
Words of a Surrogate	31
A Kind of Love Poem	32
Two Texas Incidents	33
Vignette on the 65 Bus	35
The Encounter	36
Poem for Heather	37
Sometime Personas	38
To My Father on the Occasion of His Face Being in the News	39
The Lady Who Came to the Psych Ward Dance	40
Before the Painting	41
Compassion	42
Taps	43
Broken	44
The Wind Machine	45
Beneath the Moon Illusion	46
The Value of Art	47
One of the Reasons I Still Remember You Fondly	48
The Martians Are Coming! The Martians Are Coming!	49
The Committee for Ruin	50
The Best of All Possible Worlds	51
View from Autumn	52
Holly Laura	53
The Rocking Horse	54
Notes from the Waiting Room	55

[OUR HOLDING, A HOLDING ON,]

Our holding, a holding on,
a respite from a world
made more blue than blue.
Here, slow dancing
to *Mood Indigo*, this
shared sadness binding us
as we sway. No words
to our togetherness, no
words to get in the way.
Just the melody…
as it plays.

THE MASTER PLAN

Offer me a filled silence: that which inheres
in the pause after the words have stopped;
and in return, I'll read to you from the Book of Mutterings.

You may project if you will; we hear what we need to.
The ambiguities will assist.

I do partly side with Kirsch: "language itself
fails before the most important information."

But if "the profoundest truths can only be gestured at,"

if I paint or play for you,
will you dance?

A THANK-YOU NOTE

No mermaids sang each to each as we
walked along the beach and you explained
the line, "Do I dare to eat a peach?" The sand
and the scuttering foam, that salty day,
well...

Neruda says there are only eleven subjects.
Because there are also only a number of
things we do, we are as redundant as poetry.

Old griefs are sometimes hard to let go,
when there is someone new to listen.
Three times, talking to you and watching the
waves mingle violet with green, I almost cried.

A good life always risks sentimentality.

A RESOLUTION OF DISTANCE

We are at the station at the end of the bayland boardwalk.
You stand too close as I read my revision,
the poem about the first time someone said to me,
"I love you." I hear your breathing; you hear mine.

I wonder if you know I feel I'm being tested.
I only thank you for saying I've improved the poem.
We are alone, the subject of the poem closing in.
I look out at the tall grass below me,
take slow, deep breaths, set in motion
my own calming.

I put the poem away and tell you
the times I've been here before, when I've said
things I otherwise wouldn't have.

You step away and somehow seem closer.

A DAY IN SAN FRANCISCO

We didn't stay long
in Golden Gate Park.
hardly time enough
to see the Wyeth exhibit
at the de Young:
a quick trip
to the Japanese Tea Garden,

then off by bus
and cable car
to Fisherman's Wharf.

For quite a while
we didn't eat
but walked,
watching the gulls.

There's something about
the sound of gulls,
sea and shore
and overlappings.

There was another transition,
that day:
you said Wyeth's feeling of emptiness
might become confused
with emptiness of feeling;
and it was only
after I marveled
that you laughed
(I never would have known)
and said
you'd read that
in the Examiner.

I've often
wondered since
how it happened,
running both from
and toward life,
we were in such a hurry.

Hell,
we didn't even take time
to run through the park
in slow motion.

WHAT REMAINS

The old jargon has now come down as
common speech, and here I discuss my
lifestyle and whether I
have my own space. Yet
there is still doing or not
doing, and nothing in between.
And it is always me that
I lay down to sleep.

AN EXPLANATION TO CONSIDER

Why do we remember what was
said at times of loss
and of unexpected gain?
Words sometimes do not convey
the nature of the change.
We grieve and praise
breaks in continuity,
for these remind us
we're alive.

FOR GREATER COMMISERATION

It isn't hard to show
there are no doors and windows
down in the meadow. Here
are the believers who don't belong.

Do you hear the fanfares of silence? Take care.
Remember your selective memory isn't working:
this becoming that never had a reason for beginning,
this incantation to keep away the real.

Not just to survive but to prevail,
come and be surly with me–
these white roses across a mahogany casket.
I thought of you earlier today, so I
took out the trash.

At the height of my musicality, I might be
able to play the triangle in the orchestra.
Just regular. No solos.

I'll see you at Guacamole's. We can have
some salsa there. I miss your
smirking face.

I don't remember ever having amnesia.

DESCRIPTION OF A PHYSICAL STATE

"...the disembodiment of reality...the rupture that seems determined to multiply itself between things and the feelings they produce in our minds..."–Artaud

What a crazy reason for going crazy. Here's a physical state for you: in this intimate setting, someone has just said, "I love you."

A weakness in the muscles, a curtain drawn across the senses. The other is not the other, but a source of disbelief. Arms, having their own volition, open. A quick sensation of falling: pleasant. Pressure felt on the skin is sought, maintained, to relieve and match the expected sensory image occurring in the mind before actual contact. Thought is banished; words no longer exist. A sensation localized behind the eyes shifts to the lips, to changing portions of their surface. The mind is here and elsewhere; this happens and does not. The face feels full and presents to the brain a sensation of tingling that grows until it delimits the whole body. The instantaneous ordering of things in the mind shifts both in logic and emotion. It reforms anew. Yet there is a constancy underneath:

Physical states where the real is most directly experienced, where words, classifications, order are set aside–states that unexpected words may trigger.

ONE SOLUTION

Fixed categories demand things be shoved into them,
and we still seek the right word for madness.

   This is the is of was.
   That, the was of will be.
   Between this word and that,
   time is passing so quickly.
                              I think it
strange that things are as they are, strange
there is something instead of nothing,
and also strange that these are strange.

These are not the slow draggy parts where everyone coughs:
Leaders profess what people want to hear.
Don't let them tell you how they'll divide the magic

from the art, what technology to take for granted.
Don't let them tell you you'll only stand out
when you're wrong, just some of us becoming what we want.

I flip a coin, have it never come down:
                              I am glad
certainty is over. It had become distracting.
Would life be better if we all shut up? What point is

there in what we say? Listen to this quickened absence,
as silence fills out our decisive pause.
One wish to extend the definition of... (a word

is needed here). I tell you this meanwhile will not last.
We will be grateful for friends who tell jokes.
I'm so glad this distracting certainty is over.

DISTANCING

The sea is not personified; it is the sea:
a parallel list of waves.

The Earth holds for now.

The sky is a darkling thing, full of
well-chosen consonants; it unsettles me
and makes me afraid.

On and on, and on,
before and after me.

I do not know what else to say.

DOBIE GILLIS AT THE EASEL

The skin across the bone is loose. Pale synonyms scatter
on the canvas. She shouts,
"Paint louder; I can hardly hear you."

I peel pages from an old thesaurus, select,
apply latinate words,
and three expletives, short, emphatic.

The acrylic varnish will bubble, take days to dry.
This collage is this collage. I will place it
by the half-shuttered window. Outside,

loud-winged birds scatter, slap,
slapping the slapping. The rain beats against the rain.
There is in this a loss of birds, of rain.

She tries to comfort, no use. The looseness
of skin provokes. She lifts
the corners of her eyes with tapered fingers,

smiles, says, "Wasn't I something?"
"Wrinkled skin is softer, I have heard," I say.
"Sic transit gloria Tuesday Weld," she replies.

SALAMMA LAMMA

You can tell by her eyes
she once was a great beauty.

The radio in her ear is
blasting a ballad denying
and accepting time.

She's a fast-talking gum popper, and
she calls herself Salamma Lamma Hotdam
because it has a rhythmic ring.

UNTITLED

He found a key
but it did not
fit the lock.
So he made a lock
for it to fit.
He built a door
to hold the lock
and a house
to fit the door.

And now he has the key to it all.

FRAGMENTS

I.

Through portals, crimson at the horizon.
Brass gong shimmering,
chartreuse sound.
And oranges, before Buddha,
in cobalt blue bowl.

II.

Crushed gravel
raked.
Boulders, small
and large, placed.
Brown wooden benches
and a light breeze
invite. I sit,
        listen
to distant wind chimes.

III.

There,
on a pond,
one black swan

glides.

WHAT I TELL YOU AS YOU DANCE

Please don't cry for my
lack of touching. I've just been watching
while your dancing articulates
the air. You dance more slowly now.
The last time I praised your dance
you said, "May I hug you? I
wouldn't do it
without your permission." My
reply: "What if I don't say anything
and you do anyway?"
was not meant to hurt.
Even though I'm not much
at touch, I like you. Yes.
I do. Here:
if I hug well,
will you let me know?

THINK-FEEL

He explained
and analyzed
analyzed and explained
until he couldn't feel.

She felt and emoted
emoted and felt
until she
couldn't think.

And they met
They talked

She looked
into his eyes
and told him
all the happy-sad
things she saw there.

He looked
into her eyes
and explained
retinal pigmentation.

From him,
she learned to think

From her,
he learned to feel.

"I feel I think,"
she said,
one day.

And he reached out
and touched her,
saying,
"I think I have
a feeling."

WHAT IT IS

On the bus,
in the back,
three white girls
trying to be black.

SHE'S GOING TO MAKE IT

I phoned Aunt Nonie after Uncle Mavis's funeral.
Aunt Nonie said she cries sometimes.
She got the boys to get the guns out of the house.
They said they didn't want her to remarry.
It wouldn't be too hard, she says, to find someone
with more money than she has.
She could give Larry and David their part,
and that would be that.
She gave the model railroad set away
and is throwing things out.
She's going to do
what she wants if it's
only for two weeks.
She couldn't even dust if Uncle Mavis was in a room.
He smoked cigars and had to sit with a can of room spray,
spraying once each time he blew smoke.
"That's marriage," he said. And he didn't take care of himself.
My aunt tells me she wants the song "Star Dust"
played during her funeral, when they aren't
doing other things.

KEEPING ON

The body fails, and you adjust.
Sometimes, you don't feel so old.
It's good to know people both older
and younger than you.
You never let a number do a number on you.

DOING SAD

I was happy for hours today. And it was a real
strain. So now I'm doing sad.

So, you say, you're doing sad? How sad.
Why?

I'll do sad if I please, I say. And it pleases me
to do sad.

Oh, you can laugh if you like
at the mental books I keep.
But it gets me through.

You seem to get through, too. I'm not pointing out what
you do.

So here's to you, not
how's by you. Right now,
I'm doing sad.

OUR HAVING KNOWN EACH OTHER FOR SOME TIME NOW

Are we loyal to the pachyderm?
We might re-examine our pieties:
What exactly has this tusker done for us?
Or we for him? Is there give and take?
Make no mistake. We need to talk.
But will we? And why do I ask?
To substantial music,
the elephant in the room is dancing.

FOR YOUR CONSIDERATION

Ever feel your world
is something by Escher?
Does the vanishing point
continually shift so
you can't figure out
the altered perspective?
When figure and ground
suddenly switch, how
long do you wait
till they revert?
Some would say, "Adapt, adapt.
Escher's a class act."
I take the tack
"Give me
the real world back" and
"Just where does that
stairway lead besides nowhere?"

ONE POET–AN UPDATE

Distraught, and distracted,
he's exhausted from inactivity.

His mind has grown mythic and lyric
as if on its own.

This week's answer for everything
is return to the womb.

Loosely associating, he's perversely considering writing the story
of some vivid heroine and the Murky Mist Monster; it might sell.

He blesses and abhors
the predictability language demands.

He's made a list of lyric words:
"bell," "meadow," "birds," "field,"
"dawn," "fragrant," "hill."
Therefore, he resents the ease of
what he calls hack lyricism:

> Here in the fragrant meadow
> to the sound of distant bells,
> birds sing.

Still, that's what he hears in his head.

He wants to have neither an East
nor a West Coast sensibility
nor anything specifically in between.
He would draw the view of others.
He would be outside, yet not looking in.

The language would be luminous, even translucent.
Light would come from the words and also pass through them.

The wannabe Zens
who say the full character of this or that
is that it is what it is
and that it is not...

Abstract level by abstract level,
he would hope to rise
saying both these at once
and have the "neither" heard as well.

The words support still what they get in the way of.

Begrudgingly he accepts the aphorism:
"Truth itself has appeared among humankind
in the thick of their flurrying metaphors."

He believes life is like most paintings:
it doesn't work if turned upside down.

He's taken with Holub saying science
and art don't speak to one another well
because of a lack
of common language, sensibility.

This holds—he agrees—between art, common sense;
it's even true within the arts themselves.
Despite this, Holub, he knows, urges awareness
"that we do share a common silence."

What he himself really wants to say
is between the words.

He's afraid what he writes
will sound like translation
from a language he doesn't know well.

He would like to see the poems Eliot burned.

As his serious thoughts run on, they are constantly
interspersed with various humorous and
semiserious asides.

> "Jaroslav, my dear," she says.
> "Is this why you drink only imported beer?"

> Pachelbel... My god, the man could have made
> a fortune in relaxation tapes.

His name is Sludge, and he's slimy.

Levertov, the arbiter of lines.

She says, "For some reason short men you have
to indulge."

Gottschalk would be thought an even better composer
if he had had a manager to cull out the bad.

All this shaping up isn't working; things are
really shipping out.

On occasion, children can be as profound as
any theologian.

Mumtaz Mahal,
your tomb is melting.

"Belief in reality is a subversive force."
                                –Polany

Don't let them tell you–
if you relax properly long enough,
you <u>can</u> make your mind go blank,
and the words tied to your thoughts disappear.

And when you come round, for some
after suggestion,
words flow even easier.

Knowing it's a line he will never rise to,
he quotes to himself, "There are still songs to be sung
on the other side of mankind."

Even with the motifs fixed,
the music does not play itself.

Would you heap praise or be bored if some
composer wrote only perfect mirror fugues?

Must you arrange the facts
to see what's really there?

> As for that particular approach:
> in what context would a deconstructed bomb
> explode?

He's stuck with this personal pronoun...
and the thought strikes him:

"So, who wants to be known as a recovering poet?"

(As the lady at the art museum said,
"You don't have to like everything.")

THIS I DO FOR MYSELF

I will be wise; I will put the adjectives after.
I will read and watch

only Pinterly plays.
But I shall endeavor

to remember there is a piece of French furniture,
a copy of an Henri II, I believe, and

it is said to be better
than the original.

TO THE GIRL WITH THE GOLDEN EYES

As I write of not touching
I remember
much of the touching I did
was done because I felt I should
and I loved you.

They say I'm writing better.
I write of what I haven't done.
I don't regret the not touching; it was
not not real enough for me.
I did look into
your eyes, though.

While I firm my aesthetic
I regret your golden eyes are gone.

WORDS OF A SURROGATE

Put aside the requirements of the moment,
let the clock stop. We'll have an early eternity.
Shadows in the distance have no hard edges.

The pleasures of the flesh,
the pleasures of the mind,
and the pleasures of the flesh and the mind combined.

Imagine shadows on a face in profile–a face far, near.
Now, the face turns…
the beautiful curve of cheek and brow.

To do then–do to, or with, and what?
Imagine this shadowed face imagining your face
turning. There, the thoughts.

Yes, some among us say desire can be sublime.
Relax. Already calmness takes hold.

Let–not make–the thoughts come, for someone imagines
your cheek
and brow as they turn.

A KIND OF LOVE POEM

What is caressing,
some rich whatever? Why
do you make of this
even this much? If you ask, "when,"
if I answer, "never," what of it that I've
still not learned to touch?

Say, "There will be time enough for windmills."
Am I being, now,
just too pedagogic? Now say once too often
how true love feels
and vanish
in an engulfment of logic. And yes,

perhaps it has all been unwise.
Still I'd not be with you
even if I could. Untouched, but felt,
I'd remember your eyes
and tell you good-bye
as I feel I should.

Please don't ask again,
or I'll have to go. But this once, though,
my retreat will be slow.

TWO TEXAS INCIDENTS

I.

It is 1979. I am walking with my mother and second step-father
in a wooded area near a park
in North Central Texas. They talk about setting up house,
buying a car, but not to me.
I go off alone.

I notice how a small stream
runs over the pebbles and rocks, parting at one point
into two even smaller streams.
Fascinated, I run to tell my mother, to get her
and my step-father to come and see too.

Finally, because I am persistent, they come.
The water does not flow as I said it did.
To the side, my mother asks,
"Do you think he really saw what he says?"
"It's possible," my step-father says. "It could
be different now. There are tides here, too."

"Really?" my mother says. "I'm so glad.
I worry about him. You know I'm
supposed to be crazy."
"Yes, I know," my step-father says,
"but I love you anyway."

II.

It is 2005. My mother has just died. I am in
her clean, well-ordered house
with my mother's sister.
Jim Dillon, an old boyfriend of my mother,
has come to call and to offer to buy
the house. I do not
enter into the conversation he has with
my aunt.

"I sure did love that gal," he says. My aunt
barely looks at him. "You know she was crazy."
He nods. "Yes, I know.
But I loved her anyway."

When he's gone, my aunt says, "I'm glad you
were here. If you hadn't been, he would've
been all over me." And we do not sell him the house.

Later, I regret not following him out
to shake his hand.

Yes, our lives, like streams,
diverge/ converge. Incidents
occur and sometimes
an echo resonates, restates
a theme.

VIGNETTE ON THE 65 BUS

On the 65 bus,
the pregnant woman
is with her small son.

He is resistant a little
to being told to behave.

He puts his hands
on either side
of her enlarged belly.

Embracing her,
he keeps them there
for several seconds,

then rests his head
near her waist,
looks up at her, smiles.

On this,
they are agreed.

THE ENCOUNTER

The woman with
protruding hammer toes
does not move
as an empty beer can
rolls against the back
of her shoes.
Now she turns, steps
out into the street.
And the can
continues on,
deftly turning
the corner
in the wind.

POEM FOR HEATHER

You seem satisfied with
the promise of no promises to keep;
borrowed pleasures, you say, are
a fair swap for you;

in sputtering moments of unlove,
when your happiness is melted in a spoon,
you sometimes mouth a silent scream–

before the overwhelming
well-being such a trifling
puncture.

SOMETIME PERSONAS

Sometimes, she has no dream to rest against.
Sometimes, she leads with her wound.
Sometimes, she is saved by timidity.
Sometimes, she teaches advanced tambourine.
She sometimes goes walking to listen to bees buzz.
One or two-veiled belly dancing–she can't (sometimes) decide.
Sometimes, she dances the innuendo.
On occasion, she replaces one hallucination with another.
Sometimes, she does housework while wearing her wedding dress.

Voracious Renata, Messalina Mercadante, or
Cécille Chaminade?

Sometimes, she's one; sometimes she's none; and
at other times, she's all these and more.

Sometimes, she always; sometimes, she nevers;
and sometimes, she simply sometimes.

TO MY FATHER ON THE OCCASION OF HIS FACE BEING IN THE NEWS

(in the voice of Einstein's elder son)

Father, they say when you first heard of Hiroshima,
    you muttered, "Oh, weh,"
    and seemed not otherwise upset.

When I went to visit my brother,
    the doctors told me, "Herr Einstein,
    people are beginning to use your father
    as a reason for going insane."
    My brother was the first.

I never knew if you felt responsible
    for me or my brother.
    Mother is now dead,
    and most of the Nobel money you gave us
    is gone.
    My brother, too, will die
    in an asylum.

Mother could not explain to us
    why you left.
    Now she and her black moods
    are gone.

I am an engineer,
    and you say you are proud.
    I do understand Relativity,
    but being your son,
    I say I do not when asked.
    I am told I handle it well.

Your face is often in the news.
    It makes my brother cry.

Father, they also say some years ago
    you apologized
    with tears in your eyes
    to Yukawa,
    the greatest of all Japanese physicists.

I share you with the world.

THE LADY WHO CAME TO THE PSYCH WARD DANCE

She is here. One of the men's wards is visiting,
and dance music plays.
Still, the words seem often from outside
even when she knows
they're from within.

She self-mutters unaware;
sub-vocal,
only she can hear.

Compelling, the words speak to her
of what she resists
yet variably believes.

Something's there making together go away,
and something's gone that could make it stay.
Her ventricles likely are expanding;
the eventual autopsy will reveal.

She's told they're looking,
trying to help. And they say
her being here helps them.
This only occasionally fits
with what she knows she tells herself
yet, still, inconstantly believes.

No rounding to an end, no pronouncement to cover,
nevertheless she proceeds,
no, exists for now, for the music,

for the dance.

BEFORE THE PAINTING

You stand before the painting.
Your face is a repetition of shapes. Your face
in the painting is a repetition of shapes.

In the painting, your eyes look out. Your face
folded outward, looks at me,
at yourself looking at the painting.

You would kiss yourself in this mirror,
slick acrylic lips touch slickered flesh.
In dreams, your lover has your face.

COMPASSION

I admire
the surface pattern
of your tears.

With care
I arrange their
changing forms of
light and shade

and afterward
fix them in the
bath of my
unweeping.

TAPS

My mother's mother felt
the saddest sound was taps.
She was not alone in that.
Twenty-four notes, well-played,
and people weep. She'd
lost a son in war, yet
always expected my uncle
to come walking up the walk
to the house. Taps
reminded her
this would never happen.
Still, at times, for decades,
she wept when she talked about him.
And always at the sound of taps.

BROKEN

The dragon's egg
is cracked,
the magic leaking out, as

hands ensheathed in
wrinkled gloves of flesh
caress the shell.

A dragon in embryo
remains so.

THE WIND MACHINE

The engineer tinkers in his mind.
Each possibility is checked.

Changes are tooled and lathed.
Technical and theoretical
relationships obtain.

The inner cogs of the wind machine
mesh and turn. The efficiency
coefficient holds.

And yet the wind against the skin:
how elegant the feel.

BENEATH THE MOON ILLUSION

Clannish frogs
croak, "group,
group" before
this large and orangish moon.
Now the moon rises,
smaller and high.
And faraway, the caribou
calling in the meadow
tread the turf
turned silver in the light.

THE VALUE OF ART

Monet's wife is dead. He has entered the room
where she lies. He is alone
with her only for minutes when he finds he

is watching the play of changing light on
the now dead face.

He runs from the room.

ONE OF THE REASONS I STILL REMEMBER YOU FONDLY

When I was anxious and
asked once too often
how to get to the concert at the
College of Notre Dame,
you phoned the U.S.
Geological Survey and then
gave me the exact
cartographic coordinates
for the campus itself.

Later you repeatedly asked why I
thought that was funny.

THE MARTIANS ARE COMING! THE MARTIANS ARE COMING!

While driving me back, you say flatly,
"Suggest; don't say.
You should be precise about the thing
and reticent about the feeling."
I blurt, "Nevertheless, nevertheless."

"O.K., O.K.," you say,
"nevertheless. The Martians are coming.
The Martians are coming."

As we near my home, you say,
"You live on the edge of Nowhere."
And I reply, "At the beginning of everything,
if you're coming back this way."

You tell me you used to think
the Martians had landed.
You ask, "How do you tell a human?"
I say, "You can't tell a human;
they never listen."

THE COMMITTEE FOR RUIN

The Committee for Ruin met today. They have decided that I am an uninvention of the most middle order. Unintentionally, I existed prior to my beginning. To remedy this, I am to be reinvented next Thursday at 2 p.m. on the steps of the courthouse.

Various officials will be assembled for the occasion. The Lord Mayor will take his seat conspicuously among us; others less immense will be seated in a special area to the side. Myriad latinate words will be applied to their titles.

A carefully screened group of intellectuals who are not intellectually competitive will examine me. The plausibility of my personality and appearance will be considered. Psychic and plastic surgery may be advised.

After my remaking I will take my place among those deemed fit. I will join the Committee for Ruin.

THE BEST OF ALL POSSIBLE WORLDS

When a skateboard rams your ankle, remember
how riding your bicycle both calmed and excited.
When the soccer ball rolls in the path of your car, don't
retrieve it with your fender. When
the little bastard down the block calls you
a rude name, remember you, too, once said things like that.
When diapers are wet and need changing, when
the fever is at 105 and you don't know why,
when the noise level is fast making you mutter
some long-depleted expletive,
maybe you'll discover why all you want is
your mother to call you in to dinner.

VIEW FROM AUTUMN

In autumn,
we set a maple leaf
afloat in a stream,
floating orange and brown,
a dream, of hues
in autumn blended,
of summer gone,
a season ended.

And yet I know,
as colors blend
and seasons merge,
we're not the last
to be, to love,
to have a dream,
as maple leaves
float in a stream.

HOLLY LAURA

When Holly Laura talks
the glistenings glint.
Holly Laura has a knack for clarity.

And when Holly Laura walks
the shimmerings shout.

But when she sings
Holly Laura shines.

THE ROCKING HORSE

When you started
refinishing the
rocking horse I
wondered at its
sad eyes.
All the tears
you have
are painted on
the eyes of this
wooden horse. I
say, "The horse does
not canter
in the field; it
does not foal
or sire." You
say, "It does not
feed on another's
essence or somehow
whittle away, defining
its self." As the
rocking horse
weeps, I
catch your glance
before you turn
back. One last
coat of
varnish
and we've
begun.

NOTES FROM THE WAITING ROOM

1

a

The sky is an anguished grey.
Raindrops drip.

They are metering the Universe,
charging us to breathe.

I am shaped by a changing environment.

Within the geometry of this simpler room,
solitude intrudes.

b   Remembering

In the middle of this I sit, amazed at my maundering mind.
When indelible thoughts of you come, I ponder them.

It is all a remembering.
I am appalled at my derivative self.

Except when I rise or pause, I always fall.
It is all a remembering.

c

You look like you're in a waiting room.
I fell on the way to an idea.
These are the stories that tell us when we are home.

The artist paints the space between the two women and the
fallen scarecrow.
He mistakes confusion for a mystical experience.

At times, we seem to own our depressions more.
Bad memories are the easiest to recall.
In the museum, the curved background paintings are beautiful.

d

In a flash, the sands of time have turned to glass.
Stand in the hot rain and shout, "Order in the chaos!"
The music of open spaces will soothe,

yet like a Cadillac maneuvering between smaller cars,
we can't tell if it's Telemann or Vivaldi.

e

Listen to the whispering stars.
These are but the stars of home.
Still they shine and burn away.
We take comfort before their fire.

In savage amusement
some other mouth may tell
why the brass bell rings.

Once upon an almost,
sounds of prinkish birds
filled this overweening when.

f

Is it all beyond our reach?
When gods confer,
do they discourse, dialog, or preach?

Anything that can be shaped, colored, or rearranged.
There is not enough silence,
not enough open space.

Shapes shift; colors fade; sounds merge.
The artist works.
Nothing remains the same.

2

a   *My Carapace*

The heretics are shouting again.
They collapse into fits of lucidity.

The voice of the turtle says,
"I will shed my carapace. My soft body parts
will be flailed by the elements."

I plan to walk on the ceiling.
To reach this point, I'm climbing the walls.

On the phone, her voice changes
as she pulls within herself and says good-bye.

I insist on the right to be naïve.
It creates the appearance of reality.

b

Sound-shapes rise in shadow and smoke
when your life is an exercise in serial cacophony.

We have made the drama.
You are a barren garden of delight,

and in the text of the thin morning,
you are a footnote to life.

c   *What Went Right*

The wind through the window comes curling dust motes
while flies caught by light's edge
flit back and forth buzzing.

The close edge of today receded.
That's what went right.

The bar sinister on my escutcheon
looks fine in the mirror.

Still I am swayed by
even my own sophistries.

d   The Dare

The penny whistle toots.
Deep in the water, the boat rides.

Fellow-travelers of the modern world,
behold the golden flame.

Divide up tomorrow and take what you can.
Your mythology finds no parallels in ours.

e

When you know it's a dream, but it won't go away.

The clocks have stopped, and time is dead and rotting.
That and that will get you the very best lover money can buy.
A fold of black, and the sun is gone.

Microdots and filigrees.

You move as the moon climbs.
A snake crawls across the threshold.
Dead birds are devoured.

Egyptian inscriptions.

Five cats scratch.

f

All this pondering may never resolve.
The signature is part of the composition.
This thing bristles against the flesh.
The mongoose does not always win.

g   Nevertheless

You are a pale slimness slinking,
a gratuity wondering at its worth.

Vivid images merge, gold and carmine.
Bars of grief melt and run.

Kittens lick your skin here and there.
Intense haste precedes intense calm.

The inevitable sepulcher waits.
The sound of tires on asphalt continues.

h

Webs of words catch best woven well.
The spider of the mind darts among the threads:

Ongololo, Eskimo caterpillar,
is unconcerned with onomatopoeia.

Due to technical difficulties this jagged shape
represents my father.

Mothwing could be your name
or Pigeon Feather.

I sleep in a newly made bed.

i

This blistery incident,
infinite in its pity.
For those who lie awake at night,
the dawn sounds begin.

j   *The Retrograde Motion of My Heart*

The drums beat three against four.
But I only want to bite you on the neck.

Money, incense, and a wandering mind.

Poppies floated on the wind all summer
shocking me on to love.

I will go tilting windmills no more.

3

a

We are the green-moneyed people.
We know how high up the mountain goes
and how to track a star.
Where shall we begin?

The first cause, some consider God.
The first stroke determines the brush painting.
And first impressions flavor our relationships.

When we start, we do not touch the sky.

b

The invented memories smell of wet wool.
The only one who remembers is the historian,
who dresses like a plainclothes cop.

Schiller's apples rot;
Kant's tower gets rebuilt.

At the border of wonderment
three pelicans flying in a row.

c

You, daughter of the Piltdown man,
mattress of mattresses.
In the middle of the immense you rest.

You are an answering machine calling itself,
leaving obscene messages.

I have given you samples of silence.
Now I bring you the full dish.

d   I Wonder Now

You play the rubato as arranged
and stick close to the melodic line.

You are light through stained glass.

Intimate initiations, under a harboring sky.

The yellow butterfly that I caught today has died.
I wonder now if I should mount its body on a pin.

e

I am bewitched by the sympathetic magic of your speech.
All we have is a fleeting meantime.
Every moment fails to last.

Take my hand in this in between:
let us learn together.
Each death is a library burning down.

f

The moon of your returning is waning.
They don't know what love is; that's why they always talk about
sex, not chocolate and umbrellas.

This feeling of singularity, the shock of the other.
When freedom feels like being lost,
in the moment before the picture is taken, there is life.

Whatever is is. Bless it.
I have achieved ambiguity.
It was all a very long time ago.

One purpose of religion: to know what to feel guilty about.
In this unearned moral certitude,
images form without transforming.

g   *After the Afternoon Is Over*

Nothing holds; happiness lies between loss and loss.
(This particular life is and is not a trompe-l'oeil nonpareil.)
Never reading books, only books about books.
Dissonance of opinion resolves through self-deceit.
Individual obscurities, immanent passages of time.
Whisperings of loss suffuse the air.

Interminable vanities and no exit.
This very hope is not eternal.
When hiding is over and the rains come:
this green region is only what it seems; there is
no underlying argument.
The intricate vanishings of an afternoon leave domains of silence.

h   *Tuesday's Poem*

O, caryatid under acid rain, at the prickly point of my dream
the trees talk to one another
under a gibbous moon.
Enter there until you achieve magenta.

Only the fix of your presence restores.
I sit in the corner alone now,
trying to jump-start reality.

I think I can see from here to Thursday.
My image of you crumbles as the days of the week.

i

Incipient hazards abound.
The oddity of it overwhelms.

The evening glows in the dark.
One by one, the stars burn out.

Broken effigies, shards of pottery.
All there is has a crack in it.

The confident child speaks in quick tones.

j   *Lines*

The actress plays to the contradictions.
Listen to the sizzling mist.
In a hopeless battle we have fallen.
Shore birds call.
My goat is not a unicorn.

k

At the coroner's wake,
your face is an infestation of charms.

The cat on the ziggurat
is as cold as love long gone away.

The scenes don't match in the film of your life,
when death becomes an aphrodisiac.

This stone pillow is a respite;
its shape invites hard resting.

l

The menace of personal freedom
when figure and ground suddenly shift
and what not to do becomes what to do.

If one should fade away, what then?
A pale presence hiding by subdividing.

The menace of personal freedom
when figure and ground suddenly shift
and what to do becomes what not to do.

m   *Spinning*

Sit in this room with the blues and the greens.
Earth: this thing spinning in space.
The view in the mirror is not the real world,
whatever you think.

n   *It Ends*

Shadows of sanity lengthen in the fading light;
the cocoon of self rests.
Bones beneath the skin angle in the dance; this name calls itself

Broken symmetry intrudes; the sexes meet and mate;
then silence enters in.

This white moment, this composition of light and space:
it ends with the enfolding of the old myths
and the sun
at a renewed horizon.

Acknowledgments

Blue Unicorn: The Master Plan; A Thank-You Note

Borderlands: Texas Poetry Review: The Value of Art; For Greater Commiseration; Two Texas Incidents

California Quarterly: Keeping On; Our Having Known Each Other for Some Time Now; The Lady Who Came to the Psych Ward Dance; Fragments; The Best of All Possible Worlds

Caveat Lector: Notes from the Waiting Room (published as One, Two, Three: This Passing Through); One Poet–An Update; Description of a Physical State; Words of a Surrogate; The Committee for Ruin

Empire: This I Do for Myself (published as Song of the Writer's Clone)

Encore: Compassion; The Professor/Poet; Beneath the Moon Illusion

Gems of Wisdom: A Book of Elder Poetry and Prose. (2011). Published by AgeSong and AgeSong Institute: For Your Consideration

Green's Magazine: Before the Painting; Vignette on the 65 Bus; A Resolution of Distance; She's Going to Make It; One of the Reasons I Still Remember You Fondly; Untitled

Gryphon: The Martians Are Coming! The Martians Are Coming!; Broken

Palo Alto Review: What I Tell You as You Dance; The Rocking Horse (published as The Breakthrough)

Psychopoetica: Before the Painting; To the Girl with the Golden Eyes

Reed Magazine: What It Is

San Carlos Poetry Workshop Anthology: Compassion; Think-Feel; A Day in San Francisco;

Secret Songs, II: Doing Sad; What Remains

Voices International: To My Father on the Occasion of His Face Being in the News; The Rocking Horse (published as The Breakthrough); The Wind Machine

Eighth Biennial Anthology of Premier Poets: What Remains

Ninth Biennial Anthology of Premier Poets: View from Autumn

Poet: A Day in San Francisco; Holly Laura; Poem for Heather; Salamma Lamma; The Encounter

The poem, To My Father on the Occasion of His Face Being in the News, is a dramatic monologue in the voice of Einstein's elder son. It was a winner of the Browning Society Poetry Competition and was later published by the sponsoring group.

www.ingramcontent.com/pod-product-compliance
Lightning Source LLC
Chambersburg PA
CBHW060642150426
42811CB00078B/2253/J